Old LOANHEAD

by
Craig Statham

A poem written by a local man describes Clerk Street in the early part of the twentieth century as a bustling hive of activity, 'like Gorgie, when Hearts are playing Celtic at home'. This photograph adds little credence to that claim, although the weekends were certainly a rowdy time, when workers from the nearby Clippens Oil Works at Straiton would frequent the town's bars. Such behaviour led to an explosion of temperance societies such as the Sir Wilfred Lawson Tent of Rechabites, the Dawn of Freedom Lodge of Good Templars and the Band of Hope.

First published in the United Kingdom, 2003,
by Stenlake Publishing,
Telephone / Fax: 01290 551122

ISBN 1 84033 260 3

The publishers regret that they cannot supply
copies of any pictures featured in this book.

Loanhead bairns at a Children's Day in the 1950s.

FURTHER READING

The books listed below were used by the author during his research. None of them are available from Stenlake Publishing. Those interested in finding out more are advised to contact their local bookshop or reference library.

John Cadzow, *Loanhead East Church of Scotland: A Retrospect 1858–1958*.

Loanhead Town Council, *Burgh of Loanhead, 1884–1959*.

Alan MacLaren, *The History of Loanhead Children's Day*.

Alan MacLaren, *Face to Face with Old Loanhead*.

Alan MacLaren and Jack Denholm, *A Journey Around Old Loanhead*.

Robertson Sutherland, *Loanhead: The Development of a Scottish Burgh*.

St Margaret's Catholic Church, *Loanhead 1878–1978*.

Nigel Watson, *MacTaggart Scott: A Company History 1898–1998*.

Dalkeith Advertiser.

Midlothian Journal.

Scotsman Magazine, September 1982.

The history of Loanhead and other Midlothian villages and towns can be researched at the Midlothian Local Studies Library, 2 Clerk Street, Loanhead, EH20 9DR.

ACKNOWLEDGEMENTS

This book could not have been produced without the aid of the staff of Midlothian Council's local studies library. Additional thanks go to local historian David Adams without whose help many of the stories contained here would not have come to light. Many thanks also to Patrick Prenter and Kathy Miller of MacTaggart Scott's, Ian Hunter of Hunter's Coaches and to my wife, for listening to, and putting up with, my regaling her with the stories in this book!

The author and publishers wish to thank the following for contributing photographs to this book: David Adams for page 32; Mrs Margaret Hogg for pages 10 (lower) and 42; MacTaggart Scott's Engineering Works for pages 9 and 10 (upper); East Lothian Council for pages 4, 8, 12, 14, 20 (both), 21–23, 26, 33, 34, 36 (both), 37 (upper) and 38 (lower); Midlothian Council for the inside front cover and pages 2, 6, 15, 16, 19, 24 (both), 27, 28, 39, 40, 41, 43, 44, 45, 47, 48, the inside back cover and the back cover; and St Margaret's Church, Loanhead, for page 46.

INTRODUCTION

It is unsurprising, given Loanhead's modern history, that its early history should be inextricably bound with the mining of coal. In 1528 the Sinclair family of Dryden undertook to bear part of the cost of 'winning the said haille cole of Leswaid' (Loanhead being known as 'Loanhead of Leswaid'). In 1669 these 'lands, coals and coal heughs of Loanhead' were passed to Sir John Nicolsone and in 1694 to Sir John Clerk, Baronet of Penicuik. It was Clerk who, in 1723, abandoned this seam at Edgefield for a more productive one at Mavisbank. Around the mid-nineteenth century the lands passed to R.B. Wardlaw Ramsay and soon after to the Shotts Iron Company.

Alongside his right to win the area's coal, Nicolsone was also granted the right to erect a 'mercat cross', hold a weekly market day, and an annual fair. Although no information remains regarding these events, it is likely that the market day and fair were granted in response to the area's growing agricultural significance. After the accession of Sir John Clerk's son – another Sir John – to the family estates in 1722, improvements in husbandry abounded. His reforms included the introduction of enclosures, land drainage, a horse gin and crop rotation. That his foresight and influence did not go unheeded is proven by the fact that a number of Loanhead farmers were members of the progressive Penicuik Farmers' Club.

Such progressive thought also saw the creation of the Loanhead Water Association in 1809. Prior to the creation of this institution the village had been supplied with water through timber pipes brought in by Sir John Clerk. The Water Association, however, was an expansive (and expensive) affair, bringing good water to the town in lead pipes. The association was under constant financial pressure and the growing demand for water to be piped into individual houses only succeeded in exacerbating this problem. Such problems, however, lessened after the association was taken over by the Town Council in 1892.

The history of industry in Loanhead is not restricted solely to coal mining with an agricultural footnote. Indeed, industry was, and still is, vibrant within the town. As with many towns on the River Esk in the age of the Industrial Revolution, paper-making was prevalent. Springfield Mill was built in 1742, was taken over by William Tod in 1865, and continued to function until the twentieth century. Also producing paper in the area (albeit to a lesser quality) was the Polton Mill. Similarly to the Springfield Mill it struggled financially in its early years, but its purchase by Alexander Annandale in 1798 saw great advances. In 1826, for example, it was the first mill in Scotland to introduce the revolutionary Fourdrinier paper-making machine. It remained open until 1949. Around 1880 the shale oil fields in the area led to the creation of the Straiton Oil Company (later the Clippens Oil Company) who mined to over 1,000 feet below ground. The Dickson Candle Company provided the Royal Navy with tallow candles in the late-nineteenth century, although the growing popularity of gas led to its demise. At around the same time Aitchison's Iron Foundry existed in Linden Place. The decision of Hugh Holms MacTaggart and Robert Grigor Scott to base their engineering works (MacTaggart Scott's) in Loanhead was due in part to the existence of Aitchison's. Hunter's Bus Company was founded in 1880 and, like MacTaggart Scott's, still exists today.

Such industrial growth could not be sustained without a population to support it and in the latter half of the nineteenth century the population of Loanhead began to grow substantially. From 1861 to 1884 it rose from 1,310 to over 2,000. In response to this population growth a campaign was started in 1884 to raise the village to burgh status and in June of that year this was granted. A burgh seal was decided upon, although it was only in 1952 that the Lord Lyon was asked to matriculate a traditional heraldic coat-of-arms. He denounced the old seal as 'a bogus misrepresentation'.

The self-help movements that pervaded the majority of Scottish towns and villages in the nineteenth century found a strong voice in Loanhead, driven by the success of the town's industries and the subsequent population growth. A subscription library was formed in 1818 with the aim of 'diffusing useful knowledge amongst all ranks'. The Loanhead Friendly Society, formed in 1802, was one of a number taking subscriptions in return for sickness, unemployment and funeral benefits. As the century wore on these small localised societies were replaced by national orders such as the Foresters, Irish National Foresters, Shepherds, Buffaloes, Oddfellows and Free Gardeners. In the latter half of the century the Rechabites and Good Templars both promoted their temperance ideals in the town. Social concern became a dominant theme with the Loanhead Co-operative Society being formed in 1861. It closed four years later, but was soon replaced by the vibrant Penicuik Co-operative Association which was to eventually have three stores in the town.

While all these societies have disappeared, modern Loanhead does have at least one remaining link with this bygone age. The Loanhead Children's Day has its roots in the annual festival of a local group – the Callants' Society. So popular was this event that gradually other societies began to organise their own 'Play Days' and by 1893 they had become so numerous that the Town Council decided to organise one grand festival. Apart from such festivals, the Children's Day as we know it had two forerunners – the celebrations to mark the diamond jubilee of Queen Victoria in 1897 and the coronation of King Edward VII in 1902. Perhaps due to the willingness of the organising committee to introduce changes (for example, from 1982 the use of tights and powdered wigs for boys was dispensed with and kilts introduced) the event has retained its popularity with both the children and adults of the town.

Prevalent throughout the history of the town has been its link to mining. The productive limitations of the Ramsay and Burghlee collieries, which were probably established in the eighteenth century, in conjunction with the untapped resources in the area, led to the sinking of the Bilston Glen 'super colliery' in 1952. This led to the town's largest prolonged population influx. In the twenty years from 1950 around 1,400 local authority and private houses were built. The Burghlee closed in 1964 and the Ramsay the following year, while Bilston Glen continued functioning until the aftermath of the miners' strike in 1989.

In the years after the closure of Bilston Glen the town was to enter a period of change, although its link with primary industry remained through MacTaggart Scott's engineering works. In the 1980s the building of the Edinburgh City bypass, just to the north of the town, meant that easy access to and from the town was created and, as a result, the 1990s saw the opening of a sizeable retail park and an IKEA furnishings store, both just outwith the town's boundaries but bringing many visitors. Today, Loanhead continues to grow in size, with private housing estates cementing its position as an important dormitory town for Edinburgh.

The larger houses in this part of the High Street have remained largely untouched by property development since this photograph was taken. The opening on the left leads to Mavisbank House, while the house with the small round window is the Mavisbank jointure house, probably built after Mavisbank House in the eighteenth century and certainly one of the oldest buildings in the town. A jointure house is one gifted to a woman at the time of marriage for her use after her husband's death. Legend has it that it took no small amount of manoeuvring for the dowager Lady Clerk to negotiate the narrow door frames with her hooped dresses. Now a dwelling house, it has been argued that in the interim period the house may have been a subscription school.

Mavisbank House was built between 1723 and 1739 at the behest of Sir John Clerk. With a specific style in mind, Clerk took its architect, William Adam, to England to view the work of Sir John Vanbrugh. It was originally intended to have three floors, but this idea was abandoned. Two wings were added in the 1840s, but were demolished in 1954. From the late nineteenth century until 1951 it was used as a hospital for the mentally ill and for a time was called New Saughton Hall. During this time it was a private institution and rates per annum varied from £136 for a dormitory bed to £525 for a special sitting room and special attendants. For some, this would seem to have been money well spent as a commissioner's report of 1917 noted that three patients are 'already gone and two others are about to leave fully recovered'. A fire ravaged the building in 1973 and while its demolition was averted in 1987 by the Secretary of State for Scotland, it remains empty today.

Two of the gardeners at Mavisbank House in 1914. The lady, Miss Burton, was the head gardener for many years. Each Wednesday the carter, also pictured here, would take a fattened pig to Campbell's the Butchers who would weigh and slaughter it, and the following day the appropriate monies were paid to Miss Burton. In later years Mr Campbell would recall that the pigs were always 'full of water' to make them heavier.

Most of the houses shown in this photograph of Linden Place are still standing. It is believed that the small building at the bend, now demolished, was Aitchison's Foundry. This company was present in Linden Place from as early as 1885 and was a contributing factor in the decision to base MacTaggart Scott's works in the town because of their need for metal and steel. It continued to function until around 1908.

The gas works at the junction of High Street and Arbuthnot Road in 1939. The archway in the brick building was a 'retort', used in the process of partially converting coal to gas. The coal would have been loaded into it by the 'retortman' and the gas was stored in the gas tank beyond.

The MacTaggart Scott Engineering Works (or Station Ironworks as it was originally known) was founded in 1896 by Hugh Holms MacTaggart (son of the famous Scottish painter, William MacTaggart) and Robert Grigor Scott. Frequent expansions are evidence of its early successes, but its first real boom came with the outbreak of war in 1914 as an innovative design by the firm, that saw the replacement of the hand-operated telemotor system in submarines with a more efficient hydraulically powered one, impressed those in power. The Admiralty contracts that ensued were a sign of the future direction of the company. Indeed, so successful was the works at supplying naval orders that during the Second World War it led Lord Haw Haw to threaten the town with imminent destruction. Such rhetoric was mainly due to the works' production of the cordite catapult, pictured here, which was used to launch the Swordfish seaplanes that were particularly successful at spotting German U-boats. For safety, plans of the catapult were sent to Canada where the arresting gear was made.

In 1899 a letter was sent by MacTaggart Scott's to Ferrier and Cranston, iron-founders in Penicuik, noting that, 'the railway co. give such wretched delivery'. But despite such complaints, railways were to become the primary means of transportation used by the company. Indeed, in 1937 a railway siding was built at the works. This was mainly in response to the difficulties of transporting the particularly heavy and unwieldy cordite catapults, which had to be dismantled into four separate parts and moved the short distance to Loanhead Station by lorry. Such an advance came just in time for the Second World War. Posing here, during the conflict, are the MacTaggart Scott pattern-makers. Their work towards the war effort was deemed essential and thus they were exempt from military service.

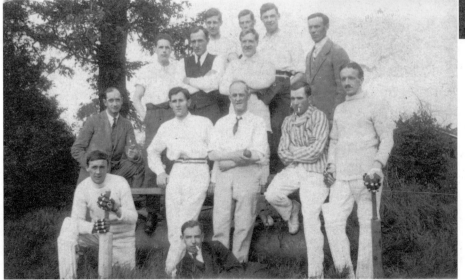

Until the 1960s the MacTaggart Scott's works boasted numerous after-work sporting teams. In addition to the cricket team pictured here (probably around the 1950s), there were football teams, a golf club, a rifle club and a fishing club. Loanhead's first cricket pitch was built in the grounds of Mavisbank House in the mid-nineteenth century and the Station Ironworks' team laid a cement wicket in Memorial Park in 1930.

The Loanhead and Roslin branch line was opened by the Edinburgh, Loanhead & Roslin Railway in July 1874. It cut a swathe through the eastern end of the town, picking up coal to deliver to Scotland's power stations. Closed to passengers on 1 May 1933, Loanhead Station remained open to freight services until the 1960s. Overlooking the line is the town's public school. After the introduction of the 1872 Education (Scotland) Act it replaced the town's subscription school and its substantial structure was erected in the place of the previous 'rickety structure'. Mr Robert Robson was retained as headmaster, although he had a tempestuous relationship with the School Board and resigned in 1897. The building remains in use as Loanhead Primary School.

The High Street was vastly redeveloped in the late 1930s and, looking towards Clerk Street, this photograph shows Loanhead in the process of this change. Only the most distant of the buildings remain and the rest have been replaced by housing, although the garden wall in the foreground still exists.

According to valuation rolls the fish restaurant at No. 34 High Street, on the immediate left, was changing hands on an almost yearly basis during the 1920s. The single storey on the opposite side of the street (just beyond the group of children) was the Tramway Stables. This had been a veterinary hospital in the last quarter of the nineteenth century and at the time of this photograph, around the 1930s, it was being used as a rifle range by the Station Ironworks' Rifle Team. Virtually every building in this photograph was demolished in the late 1950s and early '60s to make way for the town's redevelopment.

Only the building between the two sets of railings on the left remains today. Everything else in this photograph, looking along Station Road towards Clerk Street, was demolished in the late 1950s. It is believed that the tallest building (the first one beyond the railings) was, around the 1880s, the first store of the Penicuik Co-operative Association in Loanhead.

Loanhead's first bowling club was opened in 1865. Mr Leadbetter allowed the use of his garden, near the United Free Church, as a green for a rent of £2 10s per annum. Tournaments were held with prizes including the winner's portrait, a silver mounted cane, and a telescope. Competitions against neighbouring teams saw the club winning the Midlothian Bowling Club Association Trophy four times in seven years. In 1872 it was learned that the Loanhead and Roslin railway branch line was to pass through the green and the £25 compensation was distributed among the club's members. The club was closed from 1874 until 1882 when a new green – the location of this photograph – was found between The Loan and George Drive. The club attracted many eminent local characters, with Reverend Stewart and Provost Kerr sitting to the far right in the front row.

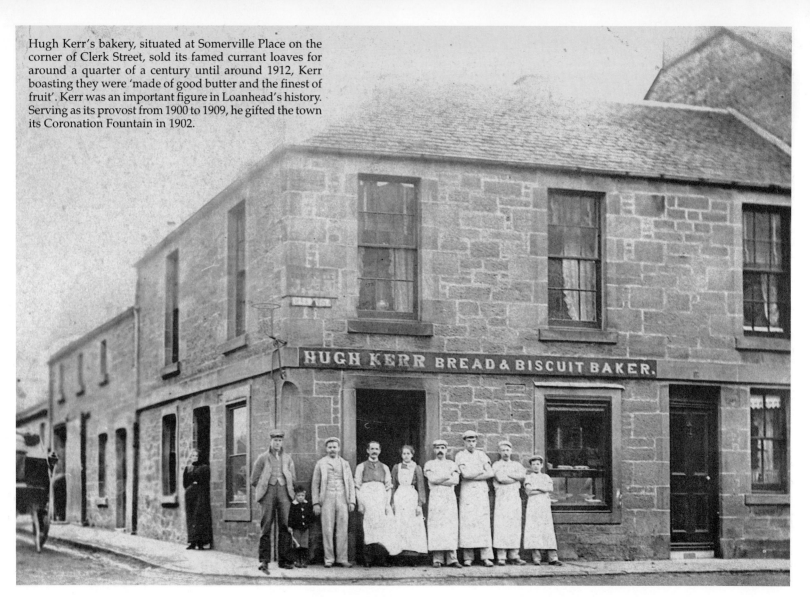

Hugh Kerr's bakery, situated at Somerville Place on the corner of Clerk Street, sold its famed currant loaves for around a quarter of a century until around 1912, Kerr boasting they were 'made of good butter and the finest of fruit'. Kerr was an important figure in Loanhead's history. Serving as its provost from 1900 to 1909, he gifted the town its Coronation Fountain in 1902.

Of these buildings in Church Street, seen here in the 1930s, only the United Free Church, built in the 1860s, remains with two or three houses. The photograph shows the recently added steeple. The church is now owned by the Lothian Gymnastics Club. The expansive Penicuik Co-operative bakehouse was one of three the society owned in Loanhead at this time. The building previously housed Hugh Kerr's bakery and was possibly also known as Pearson's Corner after the baker who had preceded Kerr. It was demolished in the early 1970s to make way for Fountain Green. Andrew Berry's shoe store (run by him for over thirty years) and the shops beyond were all demolished in the redevelopment of the early 1960s to make way for modern flats. The United Free Church had previously been the Loanhead Free Church, until its merger with the Erskine United Presbyterian Church in 1904. In 1929, after a further merger with the Church of Scotland, it became the Loanhead East Church of Scotland. During his Midlothian Campaign in 1880, William Ewart Gladstone spoke to a packed crowd in the church. According to his diary, 'Russian Aggrandisement' was the subject.

This photograph shows the United Free Church prior to the replacement of its steeple in the 1930s, due to its becoming a danger. From the late nineteenth century the church held an annual Sabbath School trip, which was eagerly awaited by the locals. Decorated carts would pick up their passengers and drive them to Habbie's Howe near Penicuik. The event continued into the twentieth century. The church also held an annual soiree at which the children would be given tea and buns, after which Mr Gillespie, an office bearer of the church, would sing songs, the theme of which was squarely focussed on religion being one's saviour: 'Intae the fecht wi' courage gang/ Wad be the burden o' my sang/ Aye dae the richt, and shun the wrang/ And ask the Lord tae help ye'.

In the late nineteenth century women were becoming increasingly aggrieved that they had little say in the running of their local co-operative stores. They responded by forming Co-operative Women's Guilds. The first was formed in Scotland in 1892 and provided women with a social outlet where they could meet with friends and discuss topical issues. This photograph shows the Loanhead branch posing for a photograph sometime after 1924, probably in the Miners' Welfare Institute Hall. It was there that they would hold their annual Burns Supper.

Many of the buildings in this photograph looking down Church Street have been demolished. The two men in bowler hats may have just attended a funeral at the old cemetery.

Many of these houses in Burghlee Terrace (known as the Back Loan) still exist today. The Brethren Hall stood on the ground to the right, behind the fence. It was recently demolished and the Brethren have moved to new meeting premises opposite Memorial Park.

All the buildings in this photograph of the High Street were demolished in the late 1950s to make way for modern flats. At numbers 9–11 can be seen the restaurant of Gerardo Massarella. This building is notable for the fact that Lord Charles Forte, founder of the Forte empire, worked in it after the First World War when it was a café owned by his uncle (possibly Giodina Macari). Years later he remembered it selling sandwiches and ice cream sundaes, and having a small billiard room with a single table. Customers could also pay to hear the shop's pianola. A newspaper advertisement from 1933 noted 'Make it a Habit and Make it Forte's Loanhead'.

The lady with the pram is crossing the road outside Robertson's tobacconist and stationer's in Clerk Street around 1939. Alexander Robertson took over the shop in the early 1870s and it remained in his family's hands until the late 1930s. It passed to the Scott family and then to Charles MacEwan in the 1970s, although it is now empty. The whole of the left-hand side of the street was demolished in the 1970s to make way for Fountain Green.

The buildings housing Morgan Berry's fruiterer's and the Mason's Arms public house are still standing. The majority of the other buildings in this photograph were demolished in the late 1950s to make way for a more substantial route through the town. The young man and lady are walking outside Edward and Louisa Brown's tailor's shop. Previously owned by the bootmaker John Allison, it passed to the Brown family during the First World War. It now houses the Bank of Scotland, but has been substantially redeveloped.

By the late 1950s the constantly growing volume of traffic passing through Loanhead meant that the High Street was proving insufficient as a thoroughfare from Lasswade to Penicuik. The result was the demolition of the building in Clerk Street (shown here facing down The Loan), which was known variously as 'The Block', 'Lee's Buildings', and 'Flanagan's Flats'.

A view of the same building after the side section was demolished. The shop which had been on the ground floor is most commonly remembered as Elizabeth Mitchell's grocery, which was open for forty years until around 1951.

The Loanhead Fountain was presented to the town in 1902 by Provost Hugh Kerr, owner of Kerr's bakery, to celebrate the coronation of King Edward VII. Cast in Glasgow by Walter MacFarlane and Co., it was 18 feet high and topped by a decorative lantern. It consisted of four drinking cups, although there were also places for horses and dogs to drink. The unveiling ceremony, although dampened by the cancellation of the coronation due to the future king's poor health, was a great success. A platform was erected for the town's officials, while 700 schoolchildren and many locals looked on as Mrs Kerr unveiled the gift. This was followed by a procession as the children and friendly societies marched to the football field, accompanied by Gilmerton Brass Band and the local Volunteer Force's pipers. Other events that day included a fancy dress cycle parade and a bonfire that saw one 'semi-intoxicated' man tumble into the fire, although little harm was done. The fountain was soon the subject of much contention, it being argued that it was a gathering place for 'Weary Willies'. The increase in traffic through this area of the town in the 1920s led to its removal, shortly after Kerr's death, in September 1933. Its final resting place has been a source of much speculation, with one local man recounting having seen it, in the 1950s, dismantled in a yard behind the Town Hall. Beyond the girl with the pram, standing at the foot of the Loan, is David Sharp's barber's shop (with red and white pole) which existed in the town during the Edwardian period.

Most of the houses visible on the left of the Loan are still standing, although flats have been erected in place of the single-storey toilet. On the opposite side of the street John Bolton, of the builders Kinsley and Bolton, cycles past David Caves' tobacconist shop. During the Second World War, Bolton appeared as a singer on the same charity bill as Sir Harry Lauder at the King's Theatre in Edinburgh.

Eyers Bros. the butchers (actually co-owned by Thomas, George and Susannah Eyers) had a shop situated at the foot of the Loan. Standing beside his van is Thomas Eyers who would deliver meat to surrounding areas such as Straiton, Burdiehouse and Damhead. Deliveries within Loanhead itself were made by an employee, John Yuill, in a horse-drawn van. The horse was stabled across the street, in the yard owned by Hunter's Coaches. The Eyers also owned a 'killing-house' in Memorial Park, although the government ended this practice during the Second World War. They stopped trading in the late 1960s, although the shop continued in business with their name above the door. The premises now house a card shop.

In the wake of the First World War, it was decided in the town to erect a memorial in memory of those local men who had been killed. In 1921, in order to raise further funds, a football match was organised between Loanhead and District Select and Heart of Midlothian. Although the final score is not known, around 2,000 people attended the game and over £30 was raised. The First World War was not the first time the youth of Loanhead had been called to fight. One local soldier, writing from a field hospital at Orange River during the Boer War, recorded that he was 'almost dead with fatigue and hunger and weariness and pain from my wounded hands and ribs' and that he had met 'several Loanhead men in the field . . . . I have not seen them since and some of them doubtless are no more.'

From the mid-nineteenth century working men's institutes became commonplace, promoting temperance, sociability, education and fraternity. Although the temperance ideal was soon abandoned (or perhaps due to this fact) institutes became increasingly popular. Opened in 1924, the Loanhead Miners' Welfare Institute was financed mainly by monies from the District Miners' Welfare Fund, although miners from Loanhead and Roslin also contributed 5d per month towards the building costs. It was run by a committee, the first president of which was Matthew Brown, a managing director at Shotts Iron Company. The institute housed a library of 700 books, a rosewood piano and billiard tables. It was fully taken advantage of during the 1926 strike. The building is now in use as a social club, attracting visitors from throughout the east of Scotland.

Shown here are bowlers at the Loanhead Welfare Institute Bowling Club, adjacent to the Institute itself which can be seen in the background, to the right of the bowling club pavilion.

In response to an ever-growing Lasswade parish, the Loanhead Parish Church was opened in 1883. Built of Straiton stone, it was designed by Hardy and Wight, architects of Edinburgh. It is of a simple cruciform design, while its interior was at the time described as 'very plain'.

Pictured here at a religious meeting around 1925 are inhabitants of the West End. The West End cottages were built in 1870 to house workers at Burghlee Colliery and this community, restricted solely to mining families, for many years saw themselves as distinct from Loanhead. From the 1920s to the 1950s they ran a second, if somewhat smaller, gala day in conjunction with the main event. However, the West End Gala Day was open only to those children who hailed from the West End.

Smith's lemonade lorry, sitting outside Sara Plummer's smallwares shop at No. 75 Clerk Street around 1939. The Plummer family worked from this shop for around 25 years. This pales, however, when compared to the tenure of those shopkeepers on either side of her. The Hay family grocery, for example, remained a fixture in the town for almost 70 years. Grocery shops were once plentiful, with sixteen in existence in Loanhead in 1905.

The original Loanhead picture house was a wooden affair and stood adjacent to Ramsay Park. It was owned by Mr Wilmot who garnered support for this venture from the Codona travelling family. The building pictured here in Clerk Street was opened on Christmas Day 1914. It is rumoured that in later years, when the equipment broke down, the owner's wife, Mrs Brodie, would regale the audience with a rendition of 'Daisy Daisy' (to a chorus of boos). Mr Brodie would then castigate the audience, telling them 'Mrs Brodie *can* sing and Mrs Brodie *will* sing.' Playing at the time of this photograph, around 1939, are *Test Pilot* with Clark Gable, Myrna Loy and Spencer Tracy, *Around the Town* with Vic Oliver, and *Judge Hardy's Children*. In 1949 the theatre was denied the right to continue showing movies on a Sunday, its licence being turned down by 998 votes to 504. The cinema was closed in the late 1950s when a fire destroyed the foyer. Somewhat ironically, this was during a screening of *A Night to Remember* (the story of the *Titanic*).

Although Clerk Street has seen little redevelopment over the years, the first three buildings on the left have all been demolished, replaced by council offices including Midlothian Library headquarters. St Margaret's Catholic school and church stands behind and beyond the railings and remain today. Opened in 1878, the church spent its formative years under the guidance of St David's Church in Dalkeith. The transition of Loanhead into a parish, however, saw Canon Edward Joseph Hannan undertake the role of the town's first priest. Hannan was a founding member of Hibernian Football Club.

Although popular since the early seventeenth century, improved tables and cues saw an explosion in the popularity of billiards in the nineteenth century. In most towns tables were to be found in the working men's institutes. Loanhead, however, had its own billiard hall – at No. 3 Clerk Street – the painted sign of which is still visible above the door today. Opened in the first decade of the twentieth century by Walter Moody, it regularly changed hands until its closure in the 1950s. Leagues were formed, pitting players from neighbouring towns against one another. In the late 1920s Loanhead Public No.1 won the Midlothian Billiard League Championship. Their success was rewarded by the award of gold medals to the members at the Harrow Hotel in Dalkeith.

Passing the Masonic Hall on the corner of Clerk Street and George Drive, around 1939, are Jimmy Adams and his son David. Established in 1876, Lodge St Leonard, No. 580, has played an integral part in the town's life ever since, although it was not until 1899 that these premises were built (they are still used by the lodge). The town also has a local Order of the Eastern Star – Glenesk Chapter, No. 109.

This Co-operative employee is delivering near the Reformed Presbyterian Church in Fountain Place, Clerk Street. This church's extensive history dates to 1707 when the congregation met in a thatched cottage at Pentland, but this building was not opened until 1875. The 'toon clock' was gifted by John White, a farmer at Edgefield. It originally had only three faces and it is rumoured that this was so that White's field workers could not see the time. In the 1950s it was decided to add a fourth face on the west side as the town extended that way. This cost £195 and was paid for by John White's grandson.

Passing the Reformed Presbyterian Church in Clerk Street is the horse-drawn bus that would drive through Loanhead on its way from Edinburgh to Roslin. The service was begun in the mid-eighteenth century and its popularity led to the opening of a booking office at Pearson's Corner. The bus pictured was introduced around 1905. Also in business at that time was Hunter's Coaches, founded in Lamb's Place in 1880 by William Hunter. Initially, its main purpose was transporting coal, but it soon began to transport passengers. Horses were replaced by motors after 1918 and during the Second World War the company's fleet was commandeered for military use. Hunter's coaches are still a common sight in the town.

This photograph shows Fountain Place, leading from Loanhead to Straiton. The white railings are still standing today (painted black), having avoided being removed during the Second World War due to their being obscured by a hedge. George Avenue was later built just beyond the position of the horse and cart.

From its opening in the 1830s this building was known as Hawthorn House. In 1898 it became 'The Edinburgh Girls' Reformatory and House of Refuge for Female Delinquents', more simply known as Dalry House. The girls, who would wear red and white striped dresses and aprons, were mainly employed in the laundering of clothes, although it was also intended to teach them 'religious truths, cooking, sewing and home work'. However, there were complaints about the excessive amounts of water being used by the institution (despite the advanced nature of Loanhead's water supply). The work was probably unpopular among the girls, two of them attempting to burn the laundry down in 1914. The Church of Scotland took over the building in 1924, with care of the aged soon emerging as their main priority. The building was renamed Loanhead Eventide Home, becoming Mayburn House later on. The home was recently closed.

This photograph shows mine workers sitting on a float around 1917, possibly as part of the Loanhead Gala Day parade. Behind is the pithead of one of Loanhead's two pits at that time, probably the Ramsay. It is likely that coal was being won from the site of the Ramsay in the eighteenth century, but it did not attain its popular name until 1850 when R.B. Wardlaw Ramsay became owner. Neither the Ramsay, or Loanhead's other pit, Burghlee, however, was extracting anywhere near the amount of coal that was possible. This led to the sinking, in 1952, of Bilston Glen Colliery.

This photograph, taken before 1965, shows workers from the Ramsay exiting the pit after a shift. It was not until 1842 that females and boys under ten years of age were barred from working underground. In 1841 Walter Kerr, a Loanhead collier, remembered seeing a newborn baby being raised to the surface in a basket.

Festivals have always played an important part in Scotland's social history. The 'Whipman's Play' and 'Bassie's Wedding', for example, were prevalent in a number of towns, while Loanhead had the 'Callant's Play'. Indeed the Comforts Committee, organised during the Second World War, prayed for the safe return of 'our Callants' (Callant being an alternative name for a Loanheadian). Such days were celebratory events that would see the town's societies march up Clerk Street with their silk banners, returning by the Loan. Its demise in the late nineteenth

century saw a rise in children's days and similar festivals, when local communities would band together and celebrate the town and its youth. Although the first Loanhead Children's Day took place in 1903, its origins, and this photograph, can be traced to Queen Victoria's diamond jubilee celebrations in 1897. These locals are congregating outside the Parish Church in the Loan, prior to a procession and sports for the town's children. A number of people, including Reverend Stewart in the centre, are looking at the camera, no doubt still an unusual sight at the end of the Victorian era.

Although such a scene would now be considered politically incorrect, these 'black and white minstrels' would have been considered perfectly innocuous when this photograph was taken on a Children's Day in the mid twentieth century.

Children's Day is an occasion when the townspeople of Loanhead, regardless of social, political or religious backgrounds, can assert their communal spirit. This photograph, taken in 1910, shows the 'gala court' standing in front of the first banner used during the occasion (there have since been two more). The court of king, queen and heralds is made up of children from all four of Loanhead's schools (Pentland School, St Margaret's School, Loanhead School and the Infant School). Overseeing the proceedings is Hugh Kerr, former provost of the town who served on its Gala Committee.

Joanna Jardine, the Children's Day Gala Queen, looks out upon the crowd during the 1914 ceremony. Standing at the fore of the stage is the 19th Midlothian (Loanhead) Scout Troop, who by this time had replaced the Boys' Brigade as 'Yeoman of the Guard' for the gala court. They wear shorts and a stetson-like hat based on that worn by Canadian troopers during the Boer War. It seems that the locals were not content with just the Children's Day. In 1911 they organised a 'Venice in Loanhead' festival. Water was poured down Clerk Street by the North British Railway Company and dammed to create a 'Grand Canal'. According to the *Midlothian Journal*, when the company removed the dam, at the end of the festivities, it led to the 'sorrow of the urchins' and the joy of the 'wives and mothers maist despairin'.

Pictured here with the 1914 Children's Day Queen, Joanna Jardine, are the Loyal Order of Ancient Shepherds, Rosslyn Castle Lodge, No. 2185, perhaps the most well known of Loanhead's friendly societies at that time. While the majority of members wear the collars that were common in most societies, some sport traditional plaid cloaks attached with a cairngorm, Tam o' Shanter bunnets, and carry crooks. At the parade these would be intertwined to form an archway. The society no longer exists.

The Irish National Foresters were formed in 1875 as a breakaway from the Ancient Order of Foresters. The order moved into Scotland on the back of the influx of Irish labour in the late Victorian era. The Eastern Star Branch, No. 122, formed in 1888, was one of three in Loanhead and had a link with St Margaret's Catholic church. Numerous other friendly societies emerged in the town at this time, many tracing their roots to early biblical or fictional texts. The most popular seems to have been the Loyal Order of Ancient Shepherds, although the Ancient Order of Foresters, the Free Gardeners and the Oddfellows were also prevalent in the town. Many of these societies would have had a silken banner similar to the one shown here and could have chosen from a number of banner-making companies to produce it for them. Most popular of these banner-makers was the world-renowned George Tutill of London.

In the late nineteenth century the Loanhead Choral Union exemplified the town's interest in music. In the 1920s a musical group called the Station Ironworks' Choir was also established. They performed at the Edinburgh Music Festival three times from 1923. In their first appearance a rendition of 'I'm going to my lonely bed' was described as lacking precision. Improvement followed and in 1925 they were awarded a merit certificate, having scored 177 points out of a possible 200. The group soon turned their talents to the field of amateur dramatics. From 1926 they staged a series of six productions in Loanhead. These were *Phillida, or Love on the Prairie*, *Indiana*, *Hong Kong*, *A Country Girl*, *The Toreador*, and *The Earl and the Girl*. Tickets cost between 1/3 and 3/- and, conducted by Anthony Doherty, they proved incredibly popular. However, lack of space in the Town Hall meant that they became impracticable and the last show was held in 1931. Pictured here are Mr Crawford and Miss Smith in a scene from *The Country Girl*. In later years the Fountain Players and the Loanhead Orchestral Society were formed. Buoyed by the enthusiasm of its conductor Alex Thorburn and secretary Gordon Hyslop, the Orchestral Society flourished. Their first concert in 1957 saw them playing Bizet's 'March' from *Carmen* and Haydn's 'Serenade for Strings', while a charity concert in aid of cancer saw them play the Usher Hall in Edinburgh.

The 1946–47 season was a good one for Loanhead Primary School football team. They beat Rosewell 4–0 to win the Drummond Cup with William Cherrie (back row, third from left) scoring all the goals. Their success is not altogether surprising given that three of the players in the front row went on to play professionally. Ian King (second from right) played for Leicester City and Malcolm Howieson (centre) for Grimsby Town. The most successful, however, was Alex Young (far left) who played for Hearts, Everton and Scotland.